Behind the Scenes

PUBLISHING
BOOKS AND MAGAZINES

SARAH MEDINA

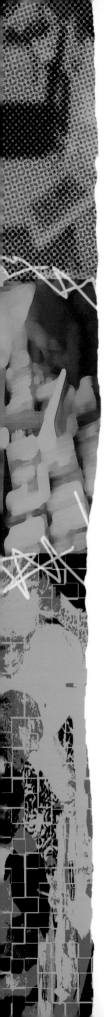

Published in 2013 by Wayland

Wayland
338 Euston Road
London NW1 3BH

Wayland Australia
Level 17/ 207 Kent Street
Sydney NSW 2000

Editor: Nicola Edwards
Design manager: Paul Cherrill
Designer: Rita Storey

British Library Cataloguing in Publication Data

Medina, Sarah, 1960 –
Magazine and book publishing. - (Behind the scenes)
1. Publishers and publishing - Vocational guidance -
Juvenile literature
I. Title
070.5'023

ISBN: 978 0 7502 6403 7

The author and publisher would like to thank the following for permission to use the images
reproduced in the book:
Ace StockLimited/Alamy p24, Helene Rogers/Alamy p19; Oli Scarff/Getty Images p6,
Gabriel BouysAFP/Getty Images p10, Chad Buchanan/Getty Images p11 and cover, Shaun
Curry/AFP/Getty, Gareth Davies/Getty Images p25, Images p5, Time & Life Pictures/Getty
Images p17; Tudor Photography pp 1, 2, 3, 7, 8, 9, 13, 14, 15, 16, 18, 20, 21, 26,
27, 28 and 29.

Printed in China

1 3 5 7 9 10 8 6 4 2

Wayland is a division of Hachette Children's Books,
an Hachette UK company.
www.hachette.co.uk

Contents

Introduction to publishing

Millions of people worldwide enjoy reading every day. People read print materials, such as newspapers, and digital materials, such as websites. Without publishing, there would be little for people to read. Publishing is all about making information and people's ideas widely available.

Publishing is the biggest sector of the UK's media industry. The publishing industry produces print and digital publications for everyone, from young babies to adults. The world would seem a very different place without it.

Publishing companies are usually called publishing houses. Many publishing houses are large, international organizations with several departments, each responsible for a different area of publishing. Others are small, with just a handful of staff.

Book publishing

Books are all around us, in schools, workplaces and homes. In the UK, more than 100,000 new books are published every year, in printed and digital form. There are more than a million titles currently available.

In our electronic age, books are still popular; people can borrow them from libraries, and buy them from bookshops and via the Internet. Books are even sold in supermarkets.

← *Through books, people can learn about all aspects of life – from art to zoology!*

Book publishing is divided into several key areas. Consumer (or trade) publishing includes illustrated and non-illustrated fiction and non-fiction books for children and adults. Non-consumer publishing includes educational publishing, for schools; academic publishing, for colleges and universities; and professional publishing, for businesses.

Magazine publishing

Magazines are popular with people of all ages. In the UK, more than 850 magazines are published every year, with each adult buying as many as 30.

Consumer magazines focus on popular culture, and include a wide range of content, including news, real-life stories, celebrity gossip and fashion. Special-interest magazines provide information about different hobbies and interests, such as knitting and model-making.

Customer magazines are published specifically for people who use a particular shop or supermarket. Business and professional magazines publish in-depth information about particular industries.

This book gives an overview of the book and magazine publishing industries, and the key jobs within them. It includes first-hand accounts of people working in publishing, and it will help you to work out whether publishing is for you.

Any questions?

What is digital publishing?

Digital publishing is publishing materials using electronic media, such the Internet, CD-ROMs, audio books and e-books. Through digital publishing, book and magazine publishing houses can reach a much bigger market.

← *E-books are just one form of digital publishing. Publishers are aiming to make downloadable books as portable as paperbacks.*

Key areas in publishing

Publishing is a creative and fast-moving career, with lots of people contact. Seeing someone reading a book or magazine that you have helped to create can be really exciting! All this makes publishing a popular – and competitive – career choice.

Publishing is very much a team effort. It is rare to find someone who can publish a book or magazine from scratch, on their own. The different processes require many different skills. This means that the publishing industry has a wide range of job opportunities.

⬆ Staff at Grazia *magazine set up this temporary office at the launch of a new shopping centre in London, giving people a behind-the-scenes look at how they work.*

Any questions ?

Are jobs in book and magazine publishing the same?

There is a lot of overlap between jobs in book publishing and magazine publishing, but there are differences, too. Job titles and responsibilities for the same jobs often vary. For example, an editor in book publishing may carry out picture research, but in magazine publishing a designer may have this responsibility.

The key areas in book and magazine publishing are editorial, design, production, marketing, and sales and rights. Individual jobs within these areas can vary a lot, depending on how much experience you have. Publishing also offers job opportunities in several other areas, including administration, human resources (HR), information technology (IT), accounts and legal.

Editorial

Editorial staff work with the ideas and words that are necessary for books and magazines to exist. They identify new publishing opportunities, doing research to make sure that people will want to buy a particular publication – and that it will be profitable.

Editors work closely with writers to make sure that the finished book or magazine is the best it can be. They help to shape ideas and content. They also check that all the language, grammar and facts in the publication are correct.

An editor's work may not be very obvious. The writer may seem to be the star of the show, but even the very best writers need editorial help and support.

It's my job!

Steph: Magazine assistant editor

"I edited non-fiction children's books for two years before moving into children's magazine publishing. I have always loved getting the text into shape, even though it takes a lot of concentration! On the magazine, I have to commission artwork and attend photo shoots, too, so I get more of a say in how it all looks."

↓ *Some editors are freelance and work from home. A freelance editor may work on projects for several different publishers at the same time.*

Design

Designers work with editorial and production staff to agree what a publication will look like. They consider everything, from its size and extent, to how much text and artwork there will be on each page and how the words and images will work together.

Some publishing houses employ picture researchers to obtain any images that are used to illustrate a publication. Illustrators create any artwork that may be needed. Designers put the text and images together to create an appealing, appropriate design. They then prepare all the materials for printing.

Production

Production staff are responsible for getting publications printed. They research all the costs involved, and they work closely with repro houses, printers and binders. They may be involved with early design decisions, for example, recommending the best kind of paper to use for a publication. Their aim is to make sure that the publication is completed on time and to the best possible standard.

Marketing

Marketing is about letting people know that a book or magazine is available to buy. Marketing staff provide information and marketing materials, such as leaflets and posters, to help sales staff to sell as many copies of a publication as possible. Marketing campaigns for new books and magazines may be huge and costly, particularly if they involve extensive advertising.

← The design of a magazine cover helps it to stand out against its competition. Magazines sometimes have free gifts on their covers to attract readers and boost sales.

Sales and rights

Publishing is an industry like any other; books and magazines are sold to make money. Sales and rights help to increase a publication's profitability.

Sales staff work face-to-face with organizations such as bookshops and newsagents, schools and businesses. Their job is to persuade the organizations to buy a particular publication, or to stock it in order to sell it to the public.

Rights staff sell permission, called rights, for another publishing house or company to use the content of a book or magazine in a different way. For example, a magazine or a book may be translated and sold in a different part of the world; a book may be turned into a film or TV programme.

Any questions

What is a book fair?

A book fair is a gathering of international publishing houses. It provides the opportunity for staff to see what is happening in the industry, and to buy and sell rights.

← *Marketing staff liaise closely with editorial and sales staff to work out the best marketing campaign for a publication. Sales staff then take publicity material such as posters and bookmarks to bookshops and work with bookshop staff to promote new titles.*

Editorial jobs

Editorial jobs vary a great deal. In short, you could say that publishers deal with ideas for books or magazines, writers put the ideas into words, and editors work with the writers' words. Different skills are needed for different jobs.

Publisher

Publishers (sometimes called commissioning editors) develop new ideas for publications, and find and work with suitable writers. In book publishing, a publisher looks after a publishing list. A magazine publisher is normally responsible for just one magazine, which may be published weekly or monthly. This is one of the most senior editorial jobs, and publishers are often held responsible for the success or failure of a book or magazine.

When a publisher has decided to go ahead with a publication, she needs to work out a budget and a schedule. She also needs to find and commission suitable writers, and agree the terms of their contract. She then works closely with the author and the whole publishing team (editors, designers and other staff) to bring the book into being.

Writer

Writers of books are normally known as authors. Most authors write a whole book, although multi-contributor books are written by more than one person. In magazine publishing, articles are written by a number of journalists. Most authors are freelance, or have other jobs and write on a part-time basis. Journalists are often employed by magazine publishers, although many contributors are freelance.

Sometimes, an author may send an unsolicited manuscript to a literary agent or to a publishing house, in

THINKING AHEAD

To work in publishing, it helps to have a passion for books and magazines. Plenty of energy is good, too! Publishing often requires you to work hard and to meet lots of deadlines.

the hope that the publisher will want to publish it. Most unsolicited manuscripts are sent in by writers of fiction. Often, especially in the area of non-fiction, a publisher has a clear idea for a book, and then commissions an author to write it.

Writing for magazines is very different from writing for books. It usually takes a long time – up to two years – for a book to be published, so authors often have more time. Magazines are published quickly, often weekly or monthly, so journalists have to work to much tighter deadlines.

↓ *JK Rowling, seen here at a signing session, spent five years writing* Harry Potter and the Philosopher's Stone. *A literary agent sent the unsolicited manuscript to 13 publishing houses before one of them accepted it. The rest is publishing history – the Harry Potter books have sold millions of copies in 65 languages.*

Editor

Editors work closely with the content – the text and images – of a book or magazine. Job titles for editors vary a lot. Desk editor, junior editor, assistant editor, house editor, deputy editor, sub-editor and managing editor are just some of the job titles used! An editor's specific responsibilities vary, too, according to how much experience they have.

More senior editors may shape the material to be published in a book or magazine by reorganizing the text, or rewriting any text that is unclear or inaccurate. This is called content editing. Less experienced editors may copy edit the content of a book or magazine, or digital materials, such as a website or CD-ROM.

Some editors brief the designer of the book or magazine. Different parts of the text may need to be treated in a different way; for example, some text may need to go into a panel (such as the 'Thinking ahead' panel on this page). It is the editor's responsibility to make sure that the designer knows about features like these.

THINKING AHEAD

Copy editing is very precise work. Editors need to have a good understanding of language and the ability to concentrate for long periods. A sharp eye for detail is essential, too; without it, a missing full stop may be lost forever!

← Billboard *magazine's Tamara Conniff interviews the actor Sean Penn about the soundtrack of the film 'Into the Wild' which he directed.* Billboard *magazine is published weekly in the USA and offers news and features about the music industry.*

Proofreader

When designers design a book or magazine, they print out sets of proofs at different stages. Editors check the different sets of proofs to make sure that all the text and artwork is in the right place, and that there are no mistakes.

The very last check of the last set of proofs is done by a proofreader. This is a very important stage. It is quite easy for an editor to miss an error, when he or she has looked many times at the same material. A proofreader is new to the project, and offers a fresh pair of eyes.

→ *Editors may work with images, as well as text. In a photo selection meeting, editors help to choose the best photos to work with the words.*

Design jobs

Designer

A designer shapes text and artwork into an appealing design for a book or magazine. The design of a publication is really important. Good design makes it clear who the publication is for – whether for children or teenagers, for example – and makes it easier and more enjoyable to read. It can also help a book or magazine to sell more copies, making it more profitable.

As with editors, a designer's responsibilities vary according to how much experience he or she has. A design manager heads up the whole design team. Design managers oversee the overall style of the publishing house's books or magazines, as well as schedules and budgets. Senior designers are often responsible for an entire publishing list, or for several books or magazines, each

year. They may set up the design for each publication, leaving more junior designers to place all the text and artwork into the electronic file.

During the design phase, designers make any changes that are requested by editors on the different sets of proofs. Once the book or magazine is ready to be printed, the designer packages up the electronic files and any artwork, and marks up a photocopy of the pages that are to be printed with any instructions that the repro house or the printer will need. The publication is now in the hands of production staff.

→

Designers need to be creative, and good at communicating with others. They also need to know their way around the software programs that are used in book design.

↑ At a covers meeting, editorial, design, sales and marketing staff get together to discuss the designs for new covers, sharing their opinions and ideas.

Some designers specialize in a particular area. A book's cover is so important to sales that some publishing houses employ designers just to work on covers.

Designers who have a good understanding of electronic media are normally employed to design digital publications, such as websites. Some designers liaise with marketing staff to produce marketing materials, such as posters and catalogues.

It's my job!

Nick: Senior designer

"When I'm designing a book, I need to get as much information as I can about it before I start. A publisher or editor tells me who the book is aimed at and what it is all about. I then use some sample text and artwork to put together some early design ideas to show them. I get lots of feedback, and I make any changes until we get a design we're all happy with."

Picture researchers

Picture researchers are responsible for finding suitable images – photos or illustrations – to include in a book or magazine. They normally follow a brief provided by the writer or editor. They also agree the terms for using the images, including the fee for the area of the world in which the publication will be available.

It is often possible for picture researchers to find researched photos in or on photo agencies' catalogues, CDs or websites. They normally select more than one option for each photo required. The editor – sometimes with the writer and designer, too – then selects the photo they want to use in the book or magazine.

Sometimes, suitable researched photos do not exist. In this case, commissioned photos may be used instead. These are photos that are taken specially for the publication in a photo shoot. The picture researcher usually works closely with the editor to choose the best possible location, people and props needed for the photo shoot. The editor may then oversee the photo shoot, so that the photos that are taken follow the brief.

← *Some picture researchers specialize in a particular area, such as cookery or art. They build up knowledge of suitable agencies, photographers and illustrators, and are always on the look-out for fresh ideas.*

Existing illustrations may be found in agencies' catalogues and on their websites. However, illustrations and diagrams often need to be created especially for a book or magazine. Picture researchers look for suitable illustrators. They may commission sample material from one or more of them. The publisher, editor or designer can then choose the most appropriate illustrator. At this stage, the editor or the designer can give the illustrator a detailed artwork brief for the illustrations or diagrams required.

Illustrators

Illustrators create illustrations or diagrams, either on paper or using a computer, for use in books or magazines. They often follow an artwork brief that is written by the writer or editor. For non-fiction material, the artwork brief may very detailed and the illustrator will be expected to follow it closely. For fiction, the illustrator may have lots of scope to interpret the text more loosely.

THINKING AHEAD

Illustrators need to be very creative and able to interpret other people's ideas in a fresh, original way. An understanding of the publishing process is important. This means that they can supply their artwork as it is needed, for example, at the right size or in the correct electronic form.

←
Author and illustrator Maurice Sendak has been working in publishing for more than 50 years. Here he is standing in front of a giant piece of artwork from his famous creation, Where the Wild Things Are.

Production jobs

Production is the part of publishing that turns electronic files into a physical book or magazine that you can pick up, hold, smell – and read! Production staff help to make this happen. They are the link between editors and designers in the publishing house and outside suppliers, such as printers and binders.

There are two main parts to the production process: pre-press (sometimes called 'repro', which is short for 'reproduction') and manufacturing. Pre-press staff are responsible for checking that the electronic files supplied by the designers are suitable and ready to be printed.

Manufacturing staff look for the most suitable materials, such as paper, and suppliers. They are responsible for briefing suppliers about the job, and making sure that the work is carried out to the highest standard and on time.

Paper, printing and binding are the most expensive elements of publishing. Manufacturing staff need to make sure that their budgets are used carefully.

In most publishing houses, it is the production director (sometimes called the production manager) who is responsible for planning schedules and budgets for different

←

The production manager is briefed by a designer about the paper engineering features that will appear in a children's pop-up book. This will help her to choose the right printer for the job.

←
Production staff work closely with printers. Sometimes, a representative from a publisher will visit a printer to check and approve the pages of a new book as they come off the press.

publications. The production director keeps up with advances in production processes, such as printing, to make sure that costs are always kept as low as possible. He or she may be involved in making decisions about the standard formats to be used for different types of books or magazines.

Other staff in the production team include production controllers and production assistants. Production controllers, helped by production assistants, see publications through the many different stages of the production process, from ordering the paper to overseeing the printing and binding. Production controllers and assistants have regular meetings with editors and designers, so they are aware of any changes to the schedule.

It's my job!

Georgina: Production manager

"I work for a small company that publishes booklets and magazines for environmental organizations. We make sure that we use paper from sustainable sources for everything we publish. My job is all about managing the whole printing process, from beginning to end. As long as there's time in the schedule, I tend to use printers in China to keep costs down. I send the printer all the files and instructions they need, deal with any ongoing queries and keep a close eye on quality standards. I'd say that my work is pretty varied and interesting!"

Marketing jobs

There is no point in creating a book or magazine if no one reads it because they do not know that it exists! In a publishing house, marketing staff make sure that potential buyers find out about future publications.

A marketing department usually has a marketing director who is responsible for the whole department. Marketing managers, marketing controllers or executives and marketing assistants make up the rest of the team. They take care of the day-to-day running of marketing campaigns.

Before a marketing campaign for a new book or magazine is agreed, marketing staff meet with editorial staff to find out all about the publication. A marketing budget is set, and marketing staff then work out the details of the campaign. Important new publications may have a large marketing campaign, designed to increase sales and profit. But all new publications need at least some marketing, so that people know that they are going to be available.

↓ *Marketing staff produce catalogues, which contain information about new and existing publications.*

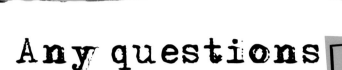

Any questions ?

What are point-of-sale materials?

Point-of-sale materials, such as posters, banners and special shelves, are often produced for larger marketing campaigns. They draw attention to a book or magazine, and encourage people to buy more copies.

→

Point-of-sale materials may be expensive, but they help to sell more copies of a publication.

In book publishing, marketing staff prepare an advance information sheet (called an AI sheet) several months before a book is published. The AI sheet, whether in printed or electronic form, provides information about the book and its author. The book's cover is designed at an early stage, too.

The AI sheet and the cover are given to sales staff, and also sent to potential customers, such as bookshop staff, who may place stock orders for the book at this stage. Once a book has been printed, copies may be sent to reviewers. A good review in the media can help to increase sales.

Sometimes, marketing staff use direct mail to market books to specific customers, such as schools and businesses. This involves sending leaflets, brochures or catalogues directly

to the customer's address. Many magazines are sold through subscription, and magazine marketing staff also use direct mail to reach these customers.

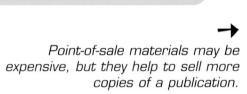

Felicity: Magazine marketing executive

"I work in magazine marketing, on the newstrade side. Newstrade is when magazines are sold in shops, rather than through subscription. Most of my work involves analysing sales of previous magazines and trying to work out ways to increase sales of the next magazine."

Sales and rights jobs

Sales and rights are two different areas of publishing. However, they both aim to achieve the same thing: to increase the amount of profit made from books and magazines. Sales staff do this by selling the physical books and magazines to customers. Rights staff sell something that you cannot hold in your hand: permission, or rights, to use the publication's content in a different way.

Sales

Some publishing houses have separate departments for home sales and export sales. Home sales means selling to customers in the UK; export sales is about selling to customers in other countries. For each area, a sales director normally plans and organizes the sales campaign for new publications. Sales managers help to run the campaign. They work closely with marketing staff to make sure that all the marketing material they need is available. They then give this to sales reps, the staff who have face-to-face contact with customers.

↑ *A sales conference is a perfect opportunity for sales staff to ask authors about their books and editorial and marketing staff about future publications, so they can sell them more effectively.*

Any questions ?

What is international licensing?

International licensing is when the rights are sold to publish a book or a magazine in another country. The magazine or book may be translated and its content may be adapted to make it more suitable for readers in the other country.

The Bologna Book Fair is held every year. Publishers from all over the world gather to buy and sell the rights to publish books specifically aimed at children.

Sales reps often live in the area in which they work. Depending on the publications they are responsible for, they may sell to a range of different customers. These may include bookshops, newsagents, supermarkets, schools, universities or businesses.

Rights

In a small publishing house, rights staff may be part of the sales department. Larger publishing houses normally have a separate rights department, with a rights manager managing a team of rights executives and rights assistants.

Rights staff sell rights to other companies. For example, they may sell rights to a company to produce a soft toy based on a character in a children's book, or to a newspaper to serialize a book. Some rights work involves buying rights, on behalf of a publisher, too –

for example, the rights to translate a foreign-language book and publish it in the UK.

It's my job!

Clare: Rights executive

"I work in the rights department of a children's book publisher. It's my ideal job – I love books and I love languages! I can speak French and Spanish and I've found both languages very useful in my job. I like dealing with clients all over the world. I especially enjoy going to the Bologna children's book fair in Italy every year, even though it can be hard work, with meetings all day and meals with clients in the evenings."

Advertising sales and events jobs

Although there is a lot of overlap between book and magazine publishing, there are some important differences, too. Advertising sales and events are areas of magazine publishing that are not part of book publishing.

Advertising sales

If you look through a magazine, you see that there are probably as many adverts as there are articles! Companies place adverts in magazines to make people aware of their products or services.

Selling advertising is an important way in which magazine publishers can make money.

Some adverts in magazines are very small. These are called classified ads, and they are often found on the last few pages of a magazine. Larger adverts, called advertising promotions, are much bigger, and may take up one or two whole pages. Different advertising sales staff deal with classified ads and with advertising promotions.

In the classified sales team, classified sales executives (normally called 'execs') sell advertising space to a range of companies, which they contact by telephone.

Classified sales executives in a busy telesales office.

Depending on the size of the publishing house, classified sales execs may sell advertising space for several magazines.

The display sales team handles advertising promotions. Display sales staff may contact a company directly or they may work with a media agency that represents a particular company. They normally set up face-to-face meetings in order to sell full-page adverts.

Events

An events department focuses on increasing brand awareness. This means making a magazine familiar to as many people as possible. To do this, events staff organize a variety of events, such as conferences and awards. As well as increasing brand awareness, an event raises money for a magazine publisher, through ticket sales, for example.

An events team is made up of an events director, who is in charge of the department, events managers and events coordinators. Events coordinators are the people who handle all the detailed arrangements for the event, such as sending out invitations and organizing venues.

Any questions

What is an advertorial?

An advertorial is a type of advert that is designed to look like a magazine article. The advertising message is hidden in the story and images, but it is effective, because the reader is drawn to read the advertorial in detail.

↑ Members of the band Fall Out Boy pose with their prize for best video at Kerrang! *magazine's annual awards event in London.*

Other jobs in publishing

Many of the jobs in book and magazine publishing are specialized. However, more general job opportunities are available, too. These include jobs in human resources (usually called HR), accounts, information technology (known as IT) and legal departments, and in administration.

Human resources

HR is all about human beings – the people who work in a book or magazine publishing house. HR staff are involved with all issues relating to staff employment, from hiring to firing. In larger publishing houses, they are responsible for organizing staff training. They can also advise employees who have work-related problems.

Accounts

Accounts staff are responsible for dealing with financial matters. These include paying suppliers, such as authors, other freelance staff, printers and binders, and receiving payments from customers who place orders for books or magazines. The accounts department is also responsible for staff pay, tax and pensions.

Information technology

The entire process of publishing, from writing to printing, depends on computers. IT staff can advise on and set up computer systems for book and magazine publishing houses. Most people who work in publishing are capable computer users – but when things go wrong, IT help staff are essential to get people up and running again quickly.

→ *Secretarial support is important in many areas of publishing. A job as a secretary can give you an excellent introduction to publishing as a business and to the skills used in the different departments.*

Legal

Legal staff give advice to other publishing staff on a range of issues. For example, they may help HR staff with queries about employment law, or they may advise an editor on whether or not text to be included in a publication is libellous. In some companies, legal staff draw up contracts, such as author contracts in a book publishing house. Legal staff in a publishing house are normally qualified lawyers.

Administration

Many jobs in publishing need administration (often called 'admin') support. Administrators do tasks that support other staff, such as typing letters and reports; photocopying; sending out documents, books and magazines; filing; and arranging meetings and trips abroad. Admin jobs are available in most publishing departments and can be a good way to get your first taste of working in the industry.

Any questions

How do I get into publishing?

Publishing jobs are in high demand and, often, people need a university degree to get a foot in the door. However, there are other ways in to the industry. Doing work experience, or working in admin, gives you experience and contacts that can lead to the job you really want.

← It's important to prepare well for a job interview. You will need to demonstrate that you have researched the publishing company and have thought about the books or magazines it publishes. Be ready to discuss your opinions and ideas.

Publishing and you

Publishing is a creative, exciting industry to work in. Being involved in creating a new book or magazine from scratch is very satisfying. Seeing 'your' publication for sale, or seeing someone reading it, gives you a real buzz.

On the down side, publishing can be stressful. There are lots of deadlines – and they are often tight! Some people work very long hours, and the financial rewards are not fantastic. So why do they do it? Because publishing is a passion, and people who work in the industry are usually passionate about books, about magazines, about information, about reading…

If you are interested in publishing, it helps to find out as much as you can about the industry. Reading this book is a good start! You will be able to find out more information from a careers office or library. The further information list on page 31 will point you in the direction of some useful books and websites.

Consider whether you prefer magazine or book publishing. Then think about whether you are interested in a specific area. For example:

- Are you keen on ideas and words? If so, editorial is probably the department for you.

- Are you interested in art, and want to use your skills in a practical way? Book and magazine design is a great way to be hands-on and creative.

Work experience is the best way to get an insight into book and magazine publishing, and can help you to get your first job in the industry.

↑ *Students at an art college. If you want to be a book or a magazine designer, an art or a design qualification will take you a long way to achieving your goal.*

- Are you confident and a people person? Marketing, sales and advertising are all about talking to and meeting people.

Research the qualities and skills you need to work in the area that interests you. For example, to be a proofreader, you need to have an excellent eye for detail, to be able to work alone and to concentrate – hard! These are qualities; they are largely to do with your personality. You also need to be able to mark up proofs. This is a skill, and it can be learned.

If book or magazine publishing is for you, then research, plan and prepare. It is a competitive world, but it is very rewarding. Do everything you can to achieve your goal. Good luck!

Any questions

Can I study publishing?

Some universities offer publishing courses, which give an overview of the industry, as well as more practical training. However, they are not essential to work in publishing. Most publishing houses offer training courses, either in-house or in publishing training centres.

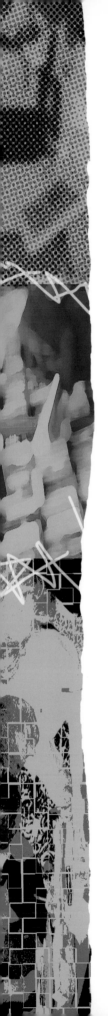

Glossary

artwork pictures used in a book or magazine, including photos, illustrations and diagrams

audio book a spoken book on a CD

binder a company that binds printed pages and a cover together to make a finished book

budget money allocated to a project

commission to choose someone to do a piece of work and tell them what is needed

commissioned photo a photo taken in a photo shoot, especially for a particular book or magazine

consumer (or trade) publishing publishing books that are sold to the general public, for example, in bookshops

contract a legal agreement, for example, between a publishing house and an author who writes a book

copy edit prepare text for publication by making sure that it is accurate and complete

digital materials published for electronic media, such the Internet and CD-ROMs

direct mail materials, such as leaflets and magazines, sent by a publishing house directly to a customer's address

e-book a book in digital form, which is read on an electronic e-book reader

employment law legal rules relating to people who work for a company or organization

extent the number of pages in a book or magazine

fiction a type of book or story written about imaginary people and events

format the size of a book or magazine

freelance when someone is self-employed and works for a company on a project-by-project basis

libellous a legal term meaning something untrue that is published and that is damaging to a person's reputation

literary agent a person who represents an author

mark up to make notes, for example, on proofs, often using special proofreading symbols

media newspapers, TV and radio

non-fiction writing that is about real people and facts

postgraduate a university course for students who have already obtained one degree

printer a company that turns electronic files from a publishing house into printed pages

proofs sets of pages used to check editorial and design matters during the process of creating a book or magazine

prop an object needed for a commissioned photo, to make the photo seem natural and realistic

repro house a company that reproduces illustrations

researched photo a photo that already exists and that can be used in a publication, often for a fee

reviewer someone who writes articles to give their opinion about something, for example, a new book

schedule a list of activities to be completed on a project, with dates by which each activity needs to be completed

serialize when a book is printed in several parts over a period of time

stock to take copies of a book or magazine to sell, for example, in a shop

subscription when someone pays for a regular order of a magazine, which is normally delivered to them by post

supplier a company that offers services to another company

unsolicited manuscript when an author's writing is sent to a publishing house even though it has not been requested

work experience a short period of time spent working for a publishing house, often without pay

Further information

The Creative and Media Industry

The creative and media industry spans a wide range of areas, from film and television to fashion and publishing. It's a highly competitive industry, because the careers it offers are seen as challenging and exciting. People who work in the industry need to combine quick-thinking and imaginative flair with tehnical skill in their chosen area. They often need to be able to work under pressure and as part of a team.

Publishing Qualifications and Training

Most people who work in book and magazine publishing go to university from school. Often, the degree subject is less important than the fact that you have got a good degree. However, for more specialist publishing areas, a specific degree subject, such as Chemistry or Accounting, can be a useful way into the industry. Some universities offer postgraduate publishing courses.

Many publishing companies offer in-house training courses. It is also possible to take short courses in different aspects of publishing
through training organizations such as The Publishing Training Centre. For information about training courses in book publishing look at:
http://www.train4publishing.co.uk/

Books

How to Get a Job in Publishing: A Really Practical Guide to Careers in Books and Magazines by Alison Baverstock, Steve Carey and Susannah Bowen (A&C Black, 2009)
Inside Book Publishing by Giles Clark and Angus Phillips (Routledge, 2008)

Websites

For general information and advice about careers, see:
http://www.connexions-direct.com/index.cfm?go=Careers

For more information about working in the publishing industry, see:
http://www.creativeskillset.org/publishing/
www.prospects.ac.uk/media_publishing_sector_overview.htm

There is information from the Publishers Association about careers in the industry at:
http://www.publishers.org.uk

The Society of Young Publishers offers support and information to people who are interested in the publishing industry. Go to:
http://www.thesyp.org.uk/

Index

Numbers in **bold** refer to pictures.